Many thanks to Hearst Magazine Media, Inc.
for permission to use quotations from Diana Vreeland's
"Why Don't You?" column from *Harper's Bazaar* magazine.

Quotations from Diana Vreeland's
autobiography, *D.V.*, are gratefully acknowledged.

Published by
Princeton Architectural Press
202 Warren Street
Hudson, New York 12534
www.papress.com

Editors: Rob Shaeffer and Stephanie Holstein
Typesetting: Paul Wagner

Library of Congress Control Number:
2021931199

# Violet Velvet Mittens

# with Everything

The Fabulous Life of

## Diana Vreeland

Written by
**Deborah Blumenthal**

Illustrated by
**Rachel Katstaller**

PRINCETON ARCHITECTURAL PRESS · NEW YORK

When I was thirteen,
I bought red lacquer for my fingernails.

"What on earth *is* that?" my mother asked.
"*Where* did you get it?"
"*Why* did you get it?"

"I want to be an exotic princess," I said.

And so it began.

I *adore* dressing up—
crimson lipstick,
face paint,
and divine outfits
can magically turn you into
a different you.

I *adore* dancing,
reading (I have a library of seven thousand books),
surfing (although I have never surfed),
ballet,
and horses.

Clothes?
I am *mad* about them.
Well, no surprise—
I was born in Paris.

And OOOOOOOH the clothes I saw!

SMASH,

CRASH,

CLASH!

Reds that were *red* reds!
Cobalt blues,
and violets
that screamed *violet*!

Growing up,
things weren't always rosy.

My mother was beautiful.
My sister Alexandra had *violet* eyes,
and *she* was beautiful.

Me?

I was extremely plain,
my mother said.

It didn't bother me *that* much.

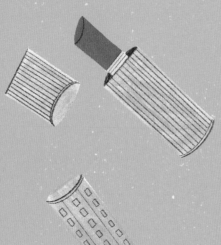

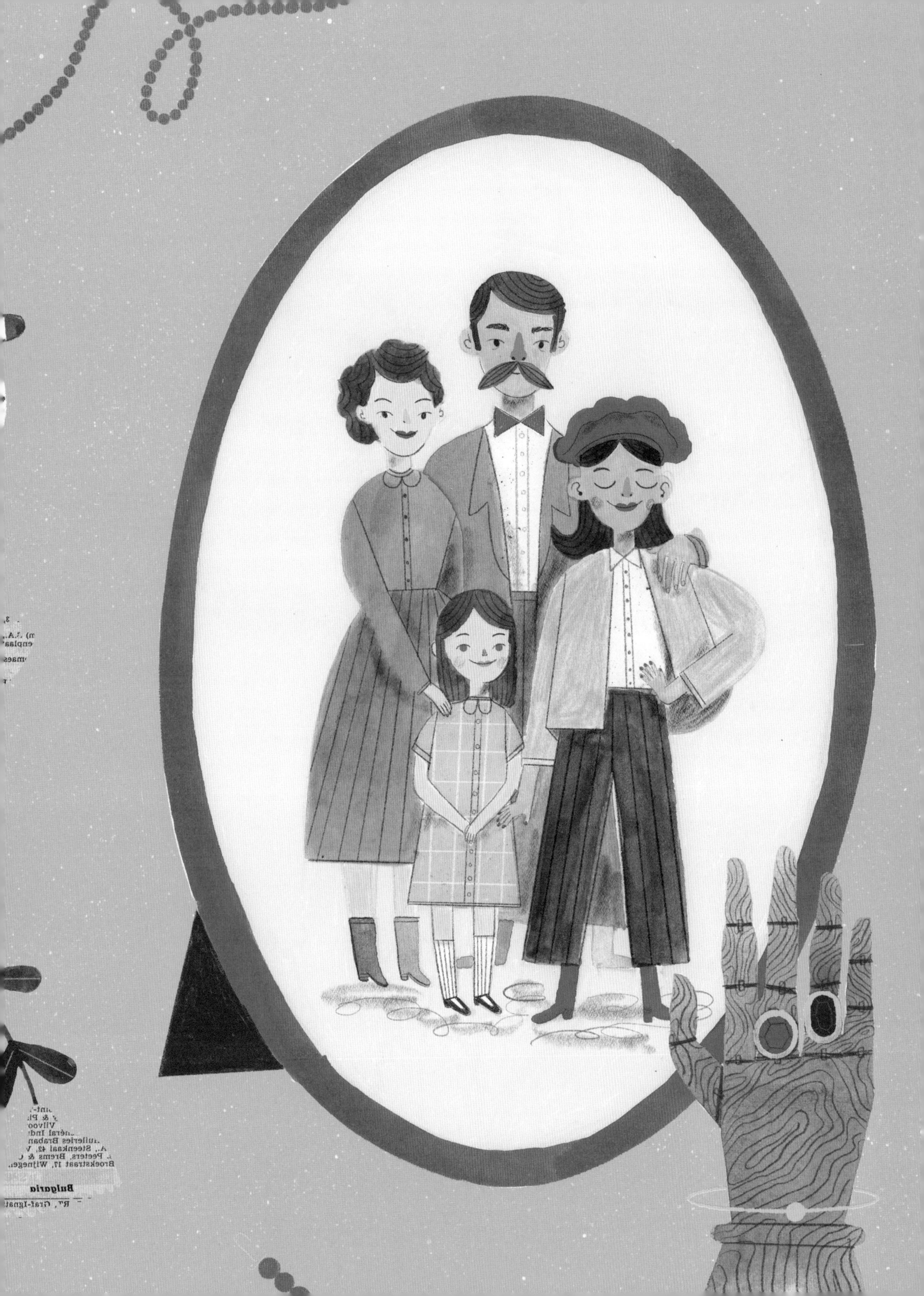
Bulgaria

I was perfectly happy when I was dancing.
That's why I was dancing *all* the time.

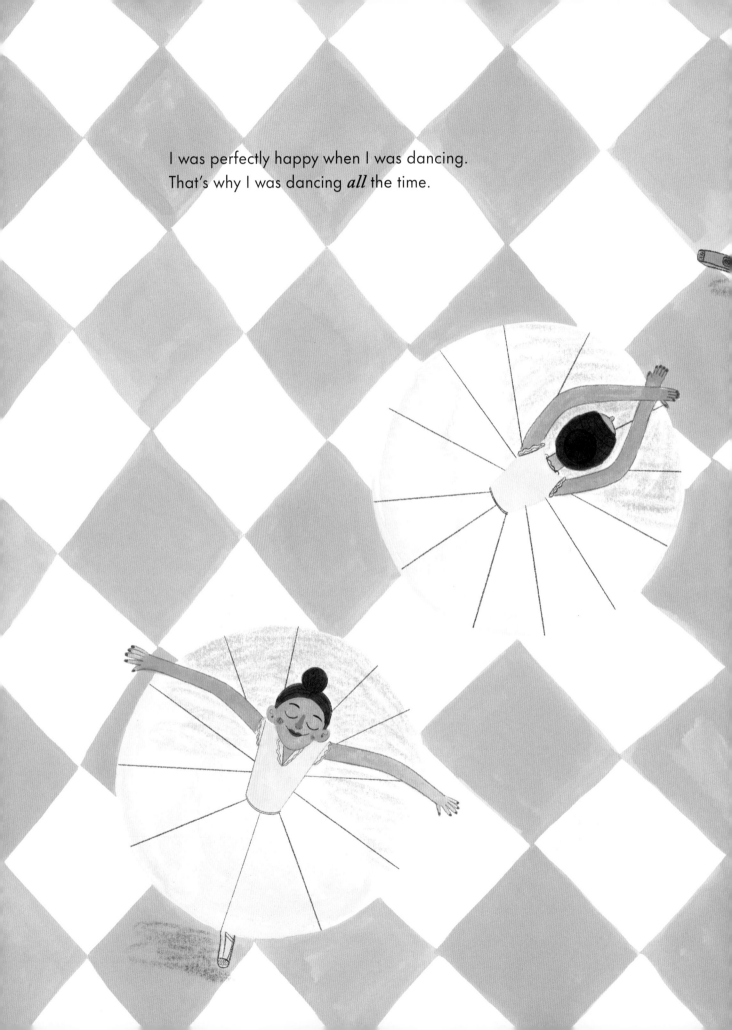

Along the way,
I found out something
*marvelous*.

Everyone who has style shares one thing:
Originality!

That means being you
and not copying anyone else.

I developed my *own* style
and became
an *Empress of Fashion*.

I am a little odd.
*E-c-c-e-n-t-r-i-c.*

But in a good way.
I like to iron my dollar bills and tissues before
they go into my handbag.

I like to make people stop
and say, *WHAT*?

Cristóbal Balenciaga, the best designer *who ever lived*,
said women didn't have to *be* perfect or beautiful
to wear his clothes—but when they did,
they *b-e-c-a-m-e* beautiful.

Alluring clothes and radiant colors
can do that.

Of course, color depends on *tone*.
And I have a lot to say about that.

Green can look like a subway car.
But the right green—a spring green—is *marvelous*!

I loathe any red with orange in it.
But I also loathe orange *without* red in it.

Then there's pale pink salmon:
I cannot *abide* that color—although, naturally,
I *adore* pink.

But make no mistake,
RED RED RED
is my *favorite* color.

Did I tell you how I got my job
at *Harper's Bazaar* magazine?

The editor in chief
saw me out dancing
in a white lace Chanel dress
with a bolero.
I had *roses* in my hair.
"You seem to know a lot about clothes," she said.

And so it began.

I started to write a column for *Harper's Bazaar*
called "Why Don't You?"
*Everybody* remembers it.

It was colorful, zany,
and *never, ever* boring.

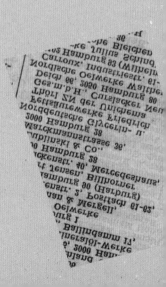

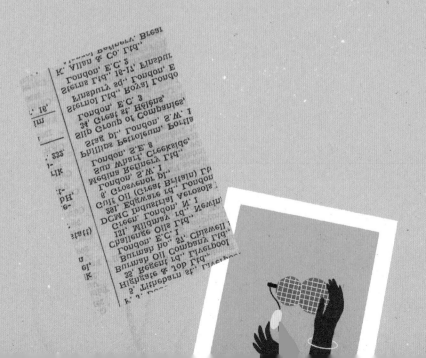

## Why Don't You…

"Put all your dogs in bright yellow collars and leads
like all the dogs in Paris?"

**Why Don't You...**

"Tie black tulle bows on your wrists?"

### Why Don't You...

"Have...the most beautiful bed imaginable, the headboard and spread of yellow satin embroidered in butterflies, alighting and flying, in every size and in exquisite colors?"

## Why Don't You...

"Have every room done up in every color green? This will take
months, years, to collect, but it will be delightful—a mélange of plants,
green glass, green porcelains, and furniture covered in sad greens,
gay greens, clear, faded, and poison greens?"

**Why Don't You...**

"Wear violet velvet mittens with everything?"

At *Harper's Bazaar*—
and later at *Vogue*,
where I was the editor in chief—
I turned fashion on its head,
dreaming up stories of glamorous worlds,
while eating peanut butter and marmalade sandwiches.

I saw things
other people didn't see.
Pink grass,
green sky,
and a scarlet sea
in a special light.

Can you imagine?

I'm also remembered for my work
at the Costume Institute of
the Metropolitan Museum of Art
in New York, changing it
from faded to *FABULOUS*.

I perfumed the air
and designed lavish fashion exhibits
to the beat of rock music.
Visitors lined up around the block.

Why?
I dared.
I dazzled.
People loved it.
And the extravagance?
It inspired them.

A *marvelous* life, for me,
is all about
being bold and inventive.

It's about dreaming
*extraordinary* dreams,
making the impossible
possible,
and *never, ever* being boring.

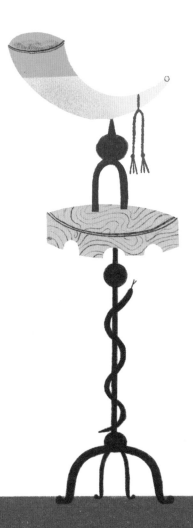

Now isn't that fun?

# More about Diana Vreeland

Diana Vreeland was a fashion diva like no other—with raven hair, red rouged cheeks, and matching scarlet nails and lips. She sounded like no one else. And she saw the world like no one else. As a style icon, fashion editor, and museum curator, Vreeland inspired generations of designers, photographers, and loyal readers to view the world through the lens of their own colorful imaginations.

She was born Diana Dalziel in Paris on September 29, 1903, during La Belle Époque, an era of French history in which artistic expression, scientific advancement, and technological innovation flourished. The daughters of a socialite and a stockbroker, Diana and her younger sister, Alexandra, were immersed in the arts, fashion, and music of the time. This exposure sparked Diana's lifelong passion for design, though her Parisian childhood came to an abrupt end in 1914, when her family emigrated to New York City to escape the onset of World War I. Once ensconced in her new city, Diana found that, even more than clothes, she was passionate about life, and she absolutely adored dancing, studying under famed Russian ballet master Michel Fokine.

But another early influence would shape her life as well. From a young age, Vreeland was haunted by the idea that she wasn't as beautiful as her mother or sister. She experienced a difficult relationship with her mother, who described her daughter as an ugly duckling. As a result, Vreeland escaped into her own vivid imagination, using bold makeup, costume, and, most of all, attitude to transform herself into an empress of fashion.

In 1924, she married banker Thomas Reed Vreeland (A man who made her feel beautiful, she said). Within a few years, the couple moved to London with their two young sons, Thomas and Frederick. While there, Vreeland opened a lingerie boutique and made frequent trips to Paris, where she befriended the top designers of the day. After six years abroad, the family returned to New York. It wasn't long before Vreeland's distinctive tastes caught the attention of fashion magazine *Harper's Bazaar*—and her quirky advice column for the modern woman titled "Why Don't You?" was born. After serving as fashion editor for more than a quarter century, Vreeland left *Harper's Bazaar* to join the staff of *Vogue*. Named editor in chief in 1963, she revolutionized the magazine by celebrating the most bizarre, outrageous, and colorful examples of the latest couture.

Vreeland seemed to have a crystal ball—an ability to show her readers the fashions they'd be wearing even before the designers had bought the fabric! On the printed page, she created a dream world through photography and graphic design. By featuring beautiful clothes and the people who wore them, she inspired readers to embrace their own striking individuality.

After nine years at *Vogue*, Vreeland was fired in 1971, reportedly due to excessive spending. In 1973, she became a special consultant to the Costume Institute of the Metropolitan Museum of Art in New York, where she organized remarkable exhibitions such as *The World of Balenciaga*, an homage to her favorite designer, Cristóbal Balenciaga, who was known for pioneering new silhouettes never before seen in women's fashion, including balloon hems and the "sack dress."

Over the course of her six-decade-long career, Vreeland imbued stories of the celebrities she had met and the far-flung places she had explored with a sense of fantasy, creating a frothy blend of fact and fiction—or "faction," as she called it. Was every story true? It didn't matter. Vreeland's imagination always took center stage.

On August 22, 1989, Diana Vreeland passed away at the age of eighty-five.

# Resources

www.dianavreeland.com

**Diana Vreeland: The Eye Has to Travel**
Directed by Lisa Immordino Vreeland, Bent-Jorgen Perlmutt,
and Frédéric Tcheng. Gloss Studio, 2011.

**D.V.**
by Diana Vreeland

**Allure**
by Diana Vreeland and Christopher Hemphill

**Diana Vreeland: Bon Mots: Words of Wisdom from the Empress of Fashion**
Edited by Alexander Vreeland and illustrated by Luke Edward Hall

**Diana Vreeland: The Modern Woman: The Bazaar Years, 1936–1962**
Edited by Alexander Vreeland

**Diana Vreeland Memos: The Vogue Years**
Edited by Alexander Vreeland

**Empress of Fashion: A Life of Diana Vreeland**
by Amanda Mackenzie Stuart